A LIFEGUIDE® BIBLE STUDY

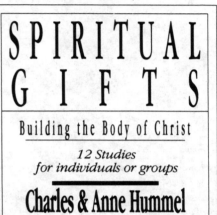

SPIRITUAL GIFTS

Building the Body of Christ

*12 Studies
for individuals or groups*

Charles & Anne Hummel

With Notes for Leaders

D1316545

INTERVARSITY PRESS
DOWNERS GROVE, ILLINOIS 60515

InterVarsity Press is the book-publishing division of InterVarsity Christian Fellowship, a student movement active on campus at hundreds of universities, colleges and schools of nursing. For information about local and regional activities, write Public Relations Dept., InterVarsity Christian Fellowship, 6400 Schroeder Rd., P.O. Box 7895, Madison, WI 53707-7895.

All Scripture quotations, unless otherwise indicated, are taken from the Holy Bible, New International Version. Copyright © 1973, 1978, International Bible Society. Used by permission of Zondervan Bible Publishers.

Cover photograph by Robert McKendrick

ISBN 0-8308-1062-5

Printed in the United States of America

Library of Congress Cataloging-in-Publication Data

Hummel, Charles E.
    Spiritual gifts: building the body of Christ: 12 studies for
  individuals or groups/Charles & Anne Hummel.
        p.   cm.—(A Lifeguide Bible study)
    ISBN 0-8308-1062-5
      1. Gifts, Spiritual—Biblical teaching.   2. Bible. N.T.—
  Criticism, interpretation, etc.   I. Hummel, Anne.   II. Title.
  III. Series.
  BS2545.G47H85   1989
  234'.13—dc20   89-15305
                                                            CIP

18	17	16	15	14	13	12	11	10	9	8	7	6	5	4
99	98	97	96	95	94	93	92							

Contents

Getting the Most from LifeGuide® Bible Studies			5
Introducing Spiritual Gifts			8
1	What Are Spiritual Gifts?	1 Corinthians 12:1-11	10
2	The Body & Its Members	1 Corinthians 12:12-31	13
3	Preparing God's People	Ephesians 4:1-16	16
4	Power for Mission	Acts 1:1-11; 2:1-13	19
5	Evangelism	Acts 2:14-41	22
6	Teaching & Preaching	Acts 18:1-28	25
7	Healing (Part 1)	Mark 1:21-45; James 5:13-20	28
8	Healing (Part 2)	John 21:1-19	31
9	Prophecy & Tongues	1 Corinthians 14:1-40	34
10	Various Spiritual Gifts	Romans 12:1-16	38
11	The Fruit of the Spirit	Galatians 5:13-26	41
12	The Excellent Way of Love	1 Corinthians 13:1-13	44
Leader's Notes			47
Appendix A: New Testament Gift Lists			60
Appendix B: The Charismatic Dimension			62

Getting the Most
from LifeGuide® Bible Studies

Many of us long to fill our minds and our lives with Scripture. We desire to be transformed by its message. LifeGuide Bible Studies are designed to be an exciting and challenging way to do just that. They help us to be guided by God's Word in every area of life.

How They Work

LifeGuides have a number of distinctive features. Perhaps the most important is that they are *inductive* rather than *deductive*. In other words, they lead us to *discover* what the Bible says rather than simply *telling* us what it says.

They are also thought provoking. They help us to think about the meaning of the passage so that we can truly understand what the author is saying. The questions require more than one-word answers.

The studies are personal. Questions expose us to the promises, assurances, exhortations and challenges of God's Word. They are designed to allow the Scriptures to renew our minds so that we can be transformed by the Spirit of God. This is the ultimate goal of all Bible study.

The studies are versatile. They are designed for student, neighborhood and church groups. They are also effective for individual study.

How They're Put Together

LifeGuides also have a distinctive format. Each study need take no more than forty-five minutes in a group setting or thirty minutes in personal study—unless you choose to take more time.

The studies can be used within a quarter system in a church and fit well in a semester or trimester system on a college campus. If a guide has more than thirteen studies, it is divided into two or occasionally three parts of approximately twelve studies each.

LifeGuides use a workbook format. Space is provided for writing answers to each question. This is ideal for personal study and allows group members to prepare in advance for the discussion.

The studies also contain leader's notes. They show how to lead a group discussion, provide additional background information on certain questions, give helpful tips on group dynamics and suggest ways to deal with problems which may arise during the discussion. With such helps, someone with little or no experience can lead an effective study.

Suggestions for Individual Study

1. As you begin each study, pray that God will help you to understand and apply the passage to your life.

2. Read and reread the assigned Bible passage to familiarize yourself with what the author is saying. In the case of book studies, you may want to read through the entire book prior to the first study. This will give you a helpful overview of its contents.

3. A good modern translation of the Bible, rather than the King James Version or a paraphrase, will give you the most help. The New International Version, the New American Standard Bible and the Revised Standard Version are all recommended. However, the questions in this guide are based on the New International Version.

4. Write your answers in the space provided in the study guide. This will help you to express your understanding of the passage clearly.

5. It might be good to have a Bible dictionary handy. Use it to look up any unfamiliar words, names or places.

Suggestions for Group Study

1. Come to the study prepared. Follow the suggestions for individual study mentioned above. You will find that careful preparation will greatly enrich your time spent in group discussion.

2. Be willing to participate in the discussion. The leader of your group will not be lecturing. Instead, he or she will be encouraging the members of the group to discuss what they have learned from the passage. The leader will be asking the questions that are found in this guide. Plan to share what God has taught you in your individual study.

3. Stick to the passage being studied. Your answers should be based on the verses which are the focus of the discussion and not on outside authorities such as commentaries or speakers. This guide deliberately avoids jumping

from book to book or passage to passage. Each study focuses on only one passage. Book studies are generally designed to lead you through the book in the order in which it was written. This will help you follow the author's argument.

4. Be sensitive to the other members of the group. Listen attentively when they share what they have learned. You may be surprised by their insights! Link what you say to the comments of others so the group stays on the topic. Also, be affirming whenever you can. This will encourage some of the more hesitant members of the group to participate.

5. Be careful not to dominate the discussion. We are sometimes so eager to share what we have learned that we leave too little opportunity for others to respond. By all means participate! But allow others to also.

6. Expect God to teach you through the passage being discussed and through the other members of the group. Pray that you will have an enjoyable and profitable time together.

7. If you are the discussion leader, you will find additional suggestions and helpful ideas for each study in the leader's notes. These are found at the back of the guide.

Introducing Spiritual Gifts

What are spiritual gifts, and what is their role in the church? Which gifts, if any, are no longer to be expected? In a day of charismatic renewal these questions draw conflicting answers.

Part of the problem is that the Holy Spirit has long been the forgotten person of the Trinity. Not that his name is unfamiliar—each Sunday millions of Christians affirm, "We believe in the Holy Spirit, the Lord, the Giver of life." But until recent decades the Spirit and his gifts have had a relatively minor place in the understanding and teaching of the church. Why has this been so?

First, the idea of a spirit is nebulous. We gain some concept of God the Father from the model of the human family. We get a picture of God the Son from the Gospel reports of Jesus. But we have difficulty wrapping our minds around the idea of God the Holy Spirit. He seems to be a ghostly kind of reality, intangible and perhaps frightening.

Second, in the biblical records the Holy Spirit does not draw attention to himself. In the Old Testament he is the Spirit of the Lord, revealing the character and purpose of God to his people. He functions as the personal presence and power of God. In the New Testament he is called the Spirit of Christ. Jesus told his twelve disciples, "He will testify about me. . . . He will not speak on his own; he will speak only what he hears. . . . He will bring glory to me" (Jn 15:26; 16:13-14). So his mission as well as his nature renders the Holy Spirit invisible.

Yet this should not put us off. The wind is also invisible. Jesus reminded Nicodemus that we don't know where it comes from or where it is going, even though we hear its sound (Jn 3:8). The wind is also powerful. It can uproot huge trees, drive sailboats through water and toss jet planes like autumn leaves.

In fact, both the Old and New Testament words for *spirit* are identical to those for wind and breath. The particular meaning, as with other words and phrases, depends on the context. Yet all three embrace life, movement, power, mystery and unpredictability.

In recent years we have become more aware of the Holy Spirit, not because his nature and mission have changed, but because of his powerful work in the church. Spiritual gifts, long neglected by theologians and people in the pew, are now a popular topic of conversation. Unexpected manifestations of the Spirit's power have occurred. Charismatic renewal is widespread and sometimes controversial. This study guide will not try to cover all aspects of the Holy Spirit's activity. Rather we will focus on the charismatic dimension which Paul refers to as "spiritual gifts" and Luke calls "filled with the Spirit."

We start with Paul's classic passage on the nature and purpose of spiritual gifts in 1 Corinthians 12. Later we will consider two other lists of gifts in Romans 12 and Ephesians 4. However, most of the studies examine specific gifts and how they build the body of Christ. Finally, the guide concludes with a study of the fruit of the Spirit, the most important of which is love.

1
What Are Spiritual Gifts?

1 Corinthians 12:1-11

T he topic of spiritual gifts can usually be counted on to stimulate vigorous discussion. What is their purpose? How should they be manifested in the church today? What should be done about certain controversial gifts which may seem divisive? This study introduces us to a vital, growing church in which spiritual gifts were prominent. Here we can begin to get answers to some of our questions.

1. As you begin this study, what questions or concerns do you have about spiritual gifts in the church today?

2. Read 1 Corinthians 12:1-11. What do we learn about the Corinthians' former religious experience (vv. 1-2)?

That they didn't know about spiritual gifts, they believed in and were influenced by idols

3. What is Paul's main point about the relationship between the Holy Spirit and what people say about Jesus Christ (v. 3)?

4. What do verses 4-6 teach about the unity and diversity of spiritual gifts?

5. In verses 7 and 11 what do we learn about the nature and purpose of spiritual gifts?

6. Paul gives a sample list of nine gifts (vv. 8-10). How would you explain the meaning of each one?

7. How might any of these gifts serve the common good in strengthening your church or fellowship group?

8. What manifestations of the Spirit have you experienced or witnessed?

What were the results?

9. Give a brief summary of what Paul has taught so far about spiritual gifts.

10. How does his teaching compare with ideas about spiritual gifts you have encountered?

2
The Body
& Its Members
1 Corinthians 12:12-31

Toody we are exposed to a variety of models for the church. The old hymn *Onward Christian Soldiers* likens it to a mighty army. Christian management manuals compare it to the modern business organization. Here the apostle Paul uses the model of the human body, a complex arrangement of many different members designed to contribute to the well-being of the whole. This passage can answer questions you might have about the ways you function in the body of Christ.

1. What different ethnic and social groups are represented in your church?

2. Read 1 Corinthians 12:12-31. What do all Christians have in common, regardless of their gifts, race or social status (vv. 12-13)?

3. Why do you think certain Christians feel inferior to others in the body of Christ (vv. 14-20)?

How does Paul encourage such people?

4. How might an attitude of superiority arise among certain members of the body (v. 21)?

5. With which group (inferior/superior) do you tend to identify? Explain.

6. According to Paul, how can we make every member of the body feel special (vv. 22-25)?

7. In what specific ways have you recently had the experience of either suffering or rejoicing with another member of the body of Christ (v. 26)?

Which do you find easier to do? Explain.

8. Notice the gifts Paul mentions in verse 28. In what way could each of those gifts contribute to the Christian community?

9. Why is it important to remember that we don't all manifest the same gifts (vv. 29-30)?

10. Verse 31 is better translated: "You are eagerly desiring the greater gifts, but now I will show you the excellent way" (to manifest them). How can the model of the body keep us from selfishly seeking what *we* consider the *greater* gifts for ourselves?

11. Describe one positive way this passage could affect relationships in your church or fellowship group.

12. What light has this passage given to your own role in the body of Christ?

3
Preparing God's People
Ephesians 4:1-16

We are accustomed to having special areas of our life taken care of by professionals: doctors, lawyers, accountants—and ministers. Most churches, in line with the professional-organizational model, expect one or more clergy to perform the necessary religious services for the laity. In this study we will compare that model with the one explained by Paul.

1. The church has been compared to a football game: twenty-two players desperately in need of rest are being watched by thousands of fans desperately in need of exercise. To what extent does this illustrate your church?

2. Read Ephesians 4:1-16. As you read through these verses, what impresses you about the kind of unity and diversity Paul desires for the church?

3. What qualities does Paul urge the Ephesians and us to exhibit (vv. 1-3)?

How would each quality build unity in a church?

4. How have you recently been able to demonstrate one of these attitudes or actions in a difficult situation?

5. In what ways do verses 4-6 stress the unity of the body of Christ?

6. Paul compares Christ to a triumphant conqueror who gives gifts (the spoils of victory) to his people (vv. 8-10). What are some of the gifts he has given (v. 11)?

7. How might each of these individuals (vv. 11-12) prepare God's people for service? (Give some practical examples from your own experience.)

8. Describe in your own words the ultimate goal Jesus Christ desires for his church (v. 13).

9. What are some marks of spiritual infancy (v. 14)?

10. Today what "winds of teaching" and "deceitful scheming" do you see blowing the church off course?

11. What does it mean to speak the *truth* in *love* (v. 15)?

How can speaking the truth in love help spiritual infants to become mature?

12. Paul states that the body grows and builds itself in love "as each part does its work" (v. 16). What "work" can you do to help the body of Christ grow?

4
Power for Mission

Acts 1:1-11; 2:1-13

Have you ever wondered how a small group of Galilean fishermen, in a remote country of the Roman Empire, were able to "turn the world upside down"? Have you also wondered how you might be effective in the church's mission? In this study we look at how Jesus empowers his followers to be his witnesses in their own country and to the far corners of the earth.

1. Describe a situation in which you felt the need to be empowered for an effective witness to Jesus Christ.

2. Read Acts 1:1-11. As he begins his second book, what does Luke say about Jesus' earlier ministry (vv. 1-3)?

3. What command and promise does Jesus give the apostles (vv. 4-5)?

4. What is foremost in their thinking now that the Lord has come back to life (v. 6)?

5. Instead of answering their question (v. 7), why do you think Jesus turns their attention back to the Holy Spirit (v. 8)?

6. What further information does Jesus give the apostles about the Holy Spirit and their mission (v. 8)?

7. Jerusalem was the capital of the region of Judea. Samaria was an adjoining region to the north. What are your "Jerusalem, Judea and Samaria" for Christian witness?

How are you carrying out a witness in your "Jerusalem"?

8. How do you think the final word from the two men affects the disciples (vv 10-11)?

9. Read Acts 2:1-13. Imagine that you are present on the day of Pentecost. Describe what you would hear and see (vv. 1-4).

10. What is the reaction of the crowd, and how do they explain this strange phenomenon (vv. 5-13)?

11. The pilgrims present on the day of Pentecost were from fourteen different geographic areas which spread out in all directions from Jerusalem. What is the purpose of the disciples' speaking in the languages of these pilgrims?

How does this event begin to fulfill Jesus' words in 1:8?

12. In what practical ways can you begin reaching beyond your Jerusalem to "the ends of the earth"?

5
Evangelism

Acts 2:14-41

The essential difference between Christianity and all other religions is the resurrection of the founder. Jesus Christ not only died and was buried, but also rose from the dead to be the living Lord of his church. No wonder, then, that Peter's first sermon featured the good news of the resurrection, not the good advice of the Sermon on the Mount. As we study Peter's message, let us be alert to how we can be more effective in presenting the good news of Christ.

1. If you were to ask your non-Christian friends to state the essence of the Christian message, what answers might they give?

2. Read Acts 2:14-41. Filled with the Spirit, Peter now speaks in the power of the Spirit. What explanation does he give to the crowd about the strange phenomenon they have heard (vv. 14-16)?

3. According to the prophet Joel, what do the events on the day of Pentecost signify (vv. 17-21)?

4. Have you ever heard what you considered to be a genuine prophecy? Explain.

What was its effect on the Christian community?

5. What did the crowd already know about Jesus, and what did they need to know (vv. 22-24)?

6. What arguments does Peter use to convince the crowd that Jesus has been raised from the dead (vv. 25-32)?

7. How are Peter's arguments, both here and earlier, well suited to the beliefs and concerns of his Jewish audience?

8. What are some of the beliefs and concerns of our society to which we can relate the gospel of Christ?

9. What connection does Peter see between Christ's resurrection and the pouring out of the Spirit on Pentecost (vv. 32-35)?

How do these two events demonstrate that Jesus is both Lord and Christ (v. 36)?

10. In your own words explain the command and promise Peter gives to the people who were "cut to the heart" by his sermon (vv. 37-41)?

11. Look back over Peter's sermon. What can we learn from this evangelist about both the *method* we use and the *message* we present today?

12. Take time to pray for several of your non-Christian friends. Ask the Lord to provide an opportunity to share the gospel with one of them this week.

6
Teaching
& Preaching
Acts 18:1-28

Why do many who start the Christian life fail to become mature believers? One reason is a lack of consistent teaching. On his missionary journeys the apostle Paul not only preached the gospel of Christ but also took pains to provide his disciples with thorough instruction in the faith. In Acts 18 we see how those who are taught can begin to pass on the teaching they have received.

1. As you think of those who have taught you the Scriptures over the years, whose ministry do you especially appreciate? Why?

2. Read Acts 18:1-28. What different types of preaching and teaching ministries does Paul have in Corinth (vv. 1-11)?

3. What do we learn about Aquila and Priscilla as they come into the orbit of Paul's ministry (vv. 1-4)?

4. How can Paul, supporting himself as a tentmaker (v. 3), be an example for us in using the gift of teaching?

5. Why do you think Paul's teaching provoked such opposition (vv. 6, 12-17)?

6. As we preach the gospel and teach the Scriptures, what aspects of our message might provoke opposition today?

7. How would the Lord's words in a vision have encouraged Paul (vv. 9-10)?

8. After spending more than a year and a half in Corinth, what places did Paul visit, and why (vv. 18-23)?

9. What guidelines can we use to determine how much time to spend teaching an individual or group—and when it's time to move on?

10. What does Luke tell us about Apollos, who appears on the scene in verses 24-25?

11. As a result of their long discipleship with Paul, how were Priscilla and Aquila able to help Apollos (v. 26)?

12. What were the results of this discipling in the ministry of Apollos (vv. 27-28)?

13. What experience have you had with teaching a new Christian who needed further instruction in the faith?

14. What basic biblical teachings are most needed in today's culture with its non-Christian pressures and values?

7
Healing
(Part 1)
Mark 1:21-45; James 5:13-20

Throughout the Bible God demonstrates his concern for the whole person. To Israel he proclaimed, "I am the LORD your healer" (Ex 15:26). The greeting "shalom," meaning peace, is far more than an absence of conflict; it involves inner tranquility, health, wholeness, integration of life—even when surrounded by turmoil. Jesus' concern for the whole person is demonstrated from the outset of his ministry. In the first half of Mark's gospel, as much space is devoted to Jesus' healing as to his teaching. The Lord also gave his disciples this ministry, which was then carried on by the church.

1. How do you respond when you or someone close to you becomes seriously ill?

2. Read Mark 1:21-45. Describe Jesus' actions in the synagogue and the response of the people (vv. 21-28).

3. How is the healing of Simon's mother-in-law (vv. 29-31) similar to and different from the previous miracle in the synagogue?

4. What impresses you about the people's various needs and Jesus' response to them (vv. 32-34)?

5. After such a busy day, why do you think Jesus rises so early to pray (vv. 35-39)?

How should this be an example for us?

6. What is remarkable about the way Jesus cares for the man with leprosy (vv. 40-45)?

7. How can we also meet people at the very point of their need for healing?

8. Read James 5:13-20. What does the range of situations needing prayer show us about God's concern for our lives (vv. 13-15)?

9. What advice does James give to those who are sick (vv. 14-15a)?

Have you ever taken his advice when you were sick? Why or why not?

10. What responsibility do Christians have for each other in connection with our sins (vv. 15-16, 19-20)?

11. What sins of attitude or action have a harmful effect on our physical and/or emotional health? Explain.

12. What instances have you seen of prayer for the sick or other manifestations of healing gifts?

8
Healing
(Part 2)

John 21:1-19

D r. Charles Mayo, of the Mayo Clinic, concluded that seventy-five per cent of all physical disease is related to emotional or spiritual illness. Many people, including those who have been Christians for years, suffer from emotional wounds of the past. As a result, they have feelings of guilt, anger or bitterness which need to be healed. In this study we consider Jesus' concern for a disciple who desperately needed such healing.

1. What are some of the major causes of emotional wounds in our society?

2. Read John 21:1-19. Describe the characters and setting given in verses 1-3.

3. What impresses you about Jesus' approach to his disciples in this disheartening situation (vv. 4-6)?

4. What reactions did the various disciples have to the large catch (vv. 7-8)?

5. If you had been there on the beach (vv. 9-14), how would you have responded to seeing Jesus?

6. What memories of Peter's past were evoked by the charcoal fire and Jesus' questions (vv. 15-17; see Jn 13:36-38; 18:15-18, 25-27)?

7. What memories of past hurts in your life have been triggered by a sudden sound or sight or smell?

8. How would Jesus' conversation with Peter bring not only pain but also healing?

9. If Jesus were to talk with you about some of your past hurts, what do you think he would say?

10. Why did Jesus tell Peter something about the way he would die (vv. 18-19)?

11. What do you think it may cost you to be a faithful follower of Christ?

12. In a few moments of silent prayer, picture the Lord Jesus standing by you and give him the memories of any painful experiences that still need to be healed.

9
Prophecy & Tongues
1 Corinthians 14

We often have difficulty bridging the gap between principle and practice. In chapter 12 Paul gave us extensive teaching about the nature and purpose of spiritual gifts. In this chapter he gives us practical advice on how the gifts of tongues and prophecy are to be manifested in corporate worship.

1. What are the advantages of both orderliness and spontaneity in church services?

2. Read 1 Corinthians 14. As you read through the entire chapter, what impressions do you get of the worship service in Corinth?

How would you have reacted to it if you had been present?

3. What does the gift of prophecy offer that *uninterpreted* tongues does not (vv. 1-5)?

4. How does Paul illustrate the problem of uninterpreted tongues from daily life (vv. 6-12)?

5. What does Paul recommend for those who speak in tongues (vv. 13-17)?

6. What does it mean to pray and sing both with our spirit and with our mind?*

How can we emphasize both the spirit and the mind in our corporate worship today?

7. Why is meaningful worship important not only for believers but also for unbelievers (vv. 20-25)?

To what extent would a non-Christian coming into your worship service respond, "God is really among you" (vv. 24-25)?

8. How might the model of worship mentioned in verse 26 strengthen the church?

9. What experience have you had in a meeting where everyone had the opportunity to contribute?

10. What guidelines does Paul give for using the gifts of prophecy and tongues in church (vv. 27-33, 39-40)?

11. What does Paul say about the source and authority of his teaching (v. 37), and how does he expect his readers to respond?

12. What misunderstanding or misuse of tongues and prophecy exists in some churches today?

13. How do various contemporary reactions to such abuses compare to Paul's solutions in this chapter?

---

*In verse 14 the word *unfruitful* means "unproductive" in the sense that the mind is not *producing* the message in the usual manner.

10
Various Spiritual Gifts
Romans 12:1-16

Spiritual gifts flourish in the soil of commitment to Christ and in the climate of love. In Romans 12 Paul sketches what is involved in our preparation for the manifestation of spiritual gifts. In a day when certain gifts are accorded special prominence, the list appearing in this passage may offer a few surprises.

1. What motivates you to serve Jesus Christ?

2. Read Romans 12:1-16. Describe in you own words what is involved in the commitment Paul urges in verse 1.

3. In what ways are we tempted to "conform to the pattern of this world" (v. 2)?

Give specific examples of how we can "be transformed" by the renewing of our mind.

4. How can Paul's model of different members with a variety of gifts help us have a realistic view of ourselves (vv. 3-5)?

5. In what way is each gift in verses 6-8 valuable to the body of Christ?

6. Which of these gifts seem to depend on some natural ability possessed by the individual?

7. Which gifts apparently can be manifested by anyone as the occasion requires?

8. In what ways have any of these spiritual gifts been manifested through you to strengthen, encourage or comfort others?

9. According to Paul, what are some of the ways that love—a fruit of the Spirit—should be manifested in the body (vv. 9-12)?

10. Give one recent example of how you have been able to demonstrate love to others.

11. What attitude or action in verses 14-16 do you need to cultivate in your present situation at home, work or school?

As you conclude this study, ask for the Holy Spirit's guidance and grace to grow in that area.

11
The Fruit of the Spirit
Galatians 5:13-26

Our technological society places a high premium on productivity. We are often valued and rewarded for what we produce, with little regard for the kind of people we are. The same can be true in the church. We often value charisma more than character. Yet our interest in the gifts of the Spirit must be matched with an equal concern for the fruit of the Spirit. In this study we will examine how the fruit of the Spirit contrasts with the acts of our old sinful nature.

1. How does it harm the cause of Christ when people displaying spiritual gifts also reveal serious character flaws?

2. Read Galatians 5:13-26. Identify the various actions of the Spirit.

3. What does the apostle Paul teach about the relationship between freedom and love (vv. 13-15)?

Give an example of how we can use our freedom in a loving way.

4. How does Paul describe the conflict we face in our daily life (vv. 16-18)?

5. In what area of life have you recently been able to resolve a spiritual conflict?

6. In Paul's list of sinful acts (vv. 19-21), which are attitudes or thoughts and which are actions?

7. Why is it so important for our thought life to be under the control of the Spirit?

8. Which of these symptoms of the sinful nature seem to be most prominent in modern society?

9. How would you define or illustrate each quality in Paul's list of the fruit of the Spirit (vv. 22-23)?

10. What does it mean to have crucified our sinful nature with its passions and desires (v. 24)? Give specific examples.

11. According to this passage, we *live* by the Spirit, are *led* by the Spirit, bear the *fruit* of the Spirit, and should *keep in step* with the Spirit. How do these descriptions help us understand the Spirit's multifaceted role in our lives?

12. How can Paul's teaching about the fruit of the Spirit relate to what he has said about spiritual gifts?

13. Think about which fruit is most needed in your life at present. Spend time in prayer, asking the Holy Spirit to cultivate it in you.

12
The Excellent Way of Love

1 Corinthians 13

The profound truth and literary beauty of Paul's discourse on love stir the imagination and probe the heart. This "hymn to love" is often used in wedding ceremonies. Yet it is by no means sentimental or idealistic. Here is a vital, practical link between Paul's teaching about the nature and purpose of spiritual gifts in chapter 12 and his instruction for their use in chapter 14. In this study we see how love, the most important fruit of the Spirit, acts and reacts in daily life to produce unity and strengthen the body of Christ.

1. In popular songs, poetry and everyday conversation, how is love viewed in our culture?

2. Read 1 Corinthians 13. How do verses 1-3 illustrate the crucial importance of love in the use of spiritual gifts?

3. What impresses you about Paul's portrait of love in verses 4-7?

Which are actions we initiate, and which are reactions to what others are doing?

4. How does this picture of love differ from our culture's view of love? (See question 1.)

5. What positive evidences of love have you experienced recently?

6. In what way is love different from spiritual gifts (vv. 8-10)?

7. How does Paul illustrate the difference between our present and future circumstances (vv. 11-12)?

8. How would you summarize Paul's statements about when and why spiritual gifts will cease (vv. 8-12)?

9. What will happen "when perfection comes" (v. 12), and when do you think that will occur?

10. How does it encourage you that God fully knows you and your present situation (v. 12)?

11. From what Paul has taught in this chapter, why is love greater than faith or hope (v. 13)?

12. Of all the qualities of love mentioned in this chapter, which do you need to develop most?

13. What have you appreciated most about your study of spiritual gifts?

14. What conclusions have you come to about the ways God wants to use you in building up the body of Christ?

Leader's Notes

Leading a Bible discussion can be an enjoyable and rewarding experience. But it can also be *scary*—especially if you've never done it before. If this is your feeling, you're in good company. When God asked Moses to lead the Israelites out of Egypt, he replied, "O Lord, please send someone else to do it!" (Ex 4:13).

When Solomon became king of Israel, he felt the task was far beyond his abilities. "I am only a little child and do not know how to carry out my duties. . . . Who is able to govern this great people of yours?" (1 Kings 3:7, 9).

When God called Jeremiah to be a prophet, he replied, "Ah, Sovereign LORD, . . . I do not know how to speak; I am only a child" (Jer 1:6).

The list goes on. The apostles were "unschooled, ordinary men" (Acts 4:13). Timothy was young, frail and frightened. Paul's "thorn in the flesh" made him feel weak. But God's response to all of his servants—including you—is essentially the same: "My grace is sufficient for you" (2 Cor 12:9). Relax. God helped these people in spite of their weaknesses, and he can help you in spite of your feelings of inadequacy.

There is another reason why you should feel encouraged. Leading a Bible discussion is not difficult if you follow certain guidelines. You don't need to be an expert on the Bible or a trained teacher. The suggestions listed below should enable you to effectively and enjoyably fulfill your role as leader.

Preparing to Lead

1. Ask God to help you understand and apply the passage to your own life. Unless this happens, you will not be prepared to lead others. Pray too for the various members of the group. Ask God to give you an enjoyable and profitable time together studying his Word.

2. As you begin each study, read and reread the assigned Bible passage to familiarize yourself with what the author is saying. In the case of book studies, you may want to read through the entire book prior to the first study. This will give you a helpful overview of its contents.

3. This study guide is based on the New International Version of the Bible. It will help you and the group if you use this translation as the basis for your study and discussion. Encourage others to use the NIV also, but allow them the freedom to use whatever translation they prefer.

4. Carefully work through each question in the study. Spend time in meditation and reflection as you formulate your answers.

5. Write your answers in the space provided in the study guide. This will help you to express your understanding of the passage clearly.

6. It might help you to have a Bible dictionary handy. Use it to look up any unfamiliar words, names or places. (For additional help on how to study a passage, see chapter five of *Leading Bible Discussions,* IVP.)

7. Once you have finished your own study of the passage, familiarize yourself with the leader's notes for the study you are leading. These are designed to help you in several ways. First, they tell you the purpose the study guide author had in mind while writing the study. Take time to think through how the study questions work together to accomplish that purpose. Second, the notes provide you with additional background information or comments on some of the questions. This information can be useful if people have difficulty understanding or answering a question. Third, the leader's notes can alert you to potential problems you may encounter during the study.

8. If you wish to remind yourself of anything mentioned in the leader's notes, make a note to yourself below that question in the study.

Leading the Study

1. Begin the study on time. Unless you are leading an evangelistic Bible study, open with prayer, asking God to help you to understand and apply the passage.

2. Be sure that everyone in your group has a study guide. Encourage them to prepare beforehand for each discussion by working through the questions in the guide.

3. At the beginning of your first time together, explain that these studies are meant to be discussions not lectures. Encourage the members of the group to participate. However, do not put pressure on those who may be hesitant to speak during the first few sessions.

4. Read the introductory paragraph at the beginning of the discussion. This will orient the group to the passage being studied.

5. Read the passage aloud if you are studying one chapter or less. You may choose to do this yourself, or someone else may read if he or she has been asked to do so prior to the study. Longer passages may occasionally be read in parts at different times during the study. Some studies may cover several chapters. In such cases reading aloud would probably take too much time, so the group members should simply read the assigned passages prior to the study.

6. As you begin to ask the questions in the guide, keep several things in mind. First, the questions are designed to be used just as they are written. If you wish, you may simply read them aloud to the group. Or you may prefer to express them in your own words. However, unnecessary rewording of the questions is not recommended.

Second, the questions are intended to guide the group toward understanding and applying the *main idea* of the passage. The author of the guide has stated his or her view of this central idea in the *purpose* of the study in the leader's notes. You should try to understand how the passage expresses this idea and how the study questions work together to lead the group in that direction.

There may be times when it is appropriate to deviate from the study guide. For example, a question may have already been answered. If so, move on to the next question. Or someone may raise an important question not covered in the guide. Take time to discuss it! The important thing is to use discretion. There may be many routes you can travel to reach the goal of the study. But the easiest route is usually the one the author has suggested.

7. Avoid answering your own questions. If necessary, repeat or rephrase them until they are clearly understood. An eager group quickly becomes passive and silent if they think the leader will do most of the talking.

8. Don't be afraid of silence. People may need time to think about the question before formulating their answers.

9. Don't be content with just one answer. Ask, "What do the rest of you think?" or "Anything else?" until several people have given answers to the question.

10. Acknowledge all contributions. Try to be affirming whenever possible. Never reject an answer. If it is clearly wrong, ask, "Which verse led you to that conclusion?" or again, "What do the rest of you think?"

11. Don't expect every answer to be addressed to you, even though this will probably happen at first. As group members become more at ease, they will begin to truly interact with each other. This is one sign of a healthy discussion.

12. Don't be afraid of controversy. It can be very stimulating. If you don't resolve an issue completely, don't be frustrated. Move on and keep it in mind for later. A subsequent study may solve the problem.

13. Stick to the passage under consideration. It should be the source for answering the questions. Discourage the group from unnecessary cross-referencing. Likewise, stick to the subject and avoid going off on tangents.

14. Periodically summarize what the *group* has said about the passage. This helps to draw together the various ideas mentioned and gives continuity to the study. But don't preach.

15. Conclude your time together with conversational prayer. Be sure to ask God's help to apply those things which you learned in the study.

16. End on time.

Many more suggestions and helps are found in *Leading Bible Discussions* (IVP). Reading and studying through that would be well worth your time.

Components of Small Groups

A healthy small group should do more than study the Bible. There are four components you should consider as you structure your time together.

Nurture. Being a part of a small group should be a nurturing and edifying experience. You should grow in your knowledge and love of God and each other. If we are to properly love God, we must know and keep his commandments (Jn 14:15). That is why Bible study should be a foundational part of your small group. But you can be nurtured by other things as well. You can memorize Scripture, read and discuss a book, or occasionally listen to a tape of a good speaker.

Community. Most people have a need for close friendships. Your small group can be an excellent place to cultivate such relationships. Allow time for informal interaction before and after the study. Have a time of sharing during the meeting. Do fun things together as a group, such as a potluck supper or a picnic. Have someone bring refreshments to the meeting. Be creative!

Worship. A portion of your time together can be spent in worship and prayer. Praise God together for who he is. Thank him for what he has done and is doing in your lives and in the world. Pray for each other's needs. Ask God to help you to apply what you have learned. Sing hymns together.

Mission. Many small groups decide to work together in some form of outreach. This can be a practical way of applying what you have learned. You can host a series of evangelistic discussions for your friends or neighbors. You can visit people at a home for the elderly. Help a widow with cleaning or repair jobs around her home. Such projects can have a transforming influence on your group.

For a detailed discussion of the nature and function of small groups, read *Small Group Leaders' Handbook* or *Good Things Come in Small Groups* (both from IVP).

Study 1. What are Spiritual Gifts? 1 Corinthians 12:1-11.

Purpose: To discover what the apostle Paul teaches about the nature and purpose of spiritual gifts, and then to consider several examples he lists.

Question 1. Often a study starts with an "approach" question, which is meant to be asked before the passage is read. These questions are important for several reasons.

First, they help the group to warm up to each other. No matter how well a group may know each other or how comfortable they may be with each other, there is always a stiffness that needs to be overcome before people will begin to talk openly. A good general question will break the ice.

Second, approach questions get people thinking along the lines of the topic of the study. Most people will have lots of different things going on in their minds (dinner, an important meeting coming up, how to get the car fixed) that will have nothing to do with the study. A creative question will get their attention and draw them into the discussion.

Third, approach questions can reveal where our thoughts or feelings need to be transformed by Scripture. This is why it is especially important not to read the passage before the approach question is asked. The passage will tend to color the honest reactions people would otherwise give because they are, of course, supposed to think the way the Bible does. Giving honest responses to various issues before they find out what the Bible says may help them to see where their thoughts or attitudes need to be changed.

Finally, do not expect everyone to participate at this point since at the outset some members may not be ready to speak out. Be sure to make this sharing brief so you can launch into the passage itself without delay.

Question 2. Have volunteers read aloud each of the three paragraphs.

Question 3. Commentators differ on the exact meaning of the phrase "Jesus be cursed," so don't get bogged down on this question. The main point is clear: the Holy Spirit does not lead people to say anything negative about Jesus.

Question 4. In Paul's teaching the central element in salvation is "grace" *(charis),*

God's action of unmerited favor, especially in Christ. The word *charisma* (translated "spiritual gift" or "charism") refers to a gift of grace from and through the Holy Spirit. It is not simply a natural ability or talent, like music or physical coordination, which a person possesses. Neither is it a church office or fruit of the Spirit. (See Appendix B.) The spiritual gifts in this chapter are actions of the Spirit which manifest his power to meet specific needs of the body through its members.

Question 6. Note that verse 9 should read "gifts of healings," indicating a variety of illnesses and means of healing. See Appendix A, pp. 60, for comments on the list of gifts appearing in the New Testament.

Study 2. The Body & Its Members. 1 Corinthians 12:12-31.

Purpose: To understand why we should not consider some gifts superior and others inferior.

Question 2. To facilitate the reading of this closely reasoned passage, you may want to get volunteers for the role of the narrator, foot, ear, eye, head. Allow a few seconds for the readers to locate their parts.

Note that the phrase *baptized by one Spirit* refers to the activity of the Holy Spirit in the Corinthians at the outset of their Christian life (see Tit 3:5).

Question 8. Note that the first three are not spiritual gifts but people: "Are all apostles? Are all prophets? Are all teachers?" (These will be considered at length in study 3 on Ephesians 4:1-16.) Then come five spiritual gifts, three of which appear in the list earlier in this chapter. (Helps and administration are similar to two of the gifts located in Romans 12:6-8, which we will look at in study 10.) Paul does not rank the five spiritual gifts. According to the teaching he has just given about the body, no one member or gift is more or less important in any absolute sense; its value depends on the need of the body at the moment.

Question 10. The Greek form of the verb can be translated either as a command ("desire the greater gifts") or as a description ("you are desiring the greater gifts"), depending on the context. Most translations make it a command, even though Paul has just taught that this is what they should *not* do, since each gift makes its own contribution to the body (see Appendix A: New Testament Gift Lists). "The excellent way" is not to desire what we think are the greater gifts, for our own status, but to have the motive of love for others. The second translation makes more sense and provides a natural bridge to chapter 13, which does not teach that love is better than spiritual gifts but rather that it is the essential motivation without which they have no value.

Study 3. Preparing God's People. Ephesians 4:1-16.

Purpose: To understand how all the members are to be involved in building the body of Christ in unity and love.

Question 2. Have the members take turns reading the passage aloud, a paragraph at a time.

Question 5. The word *faith* (v. 5) is not personal faith in Christ but the content of the Christian message. (See Galatians 1:23: "preaching the faith.")

Question 6. In verse 8 Paul quotes Psalm 68:18, with an alternative translation taken from certain rabbinic interpretations of his day. Instead of *received gifts from men,* the wording found in the psalm, Paul writes *gave gifts to men.* The *captives* probably mean the spiritual enemies Christ defeated at the cross. Verse 9 reminds the readers of Christ's descent to earth (his Incarnation) and his subsequent resurrection and ascension (see Phil 2:6-11). This passage doesn't explicitly teach that Christ descended into hell.

The list in verse 11 is usually lumped together with those in Romans 12 and 1 Corinthians 12 without realizing that here the gifts are people, while in the other two passages they are activities. Although any member of the body may prophesy as the Spirit enables (1 Cor 14:5, 31), a prophet is one through whom prophecies come frequently and consistently. Thus the New Testament mentions a number of prophets, such as Agabus and Philip's daughters (Acts 11:28; 21:9-10). Likewise, although any member may lead a person to Christ, an evangelist is consistently involved in people's conversion.

Note on Apostles and Prophets. Are there prophets and apostles in the church today? The answer must take account of the fact that in the New Testament these gifts serve more than one purpose.

Paul declared that the church is "built on the foundation of the apostles and prophets," through whom the Holy Spirit has revealed "the mystery of Christ" (Eph 2:20; 3:5). As witnesses of the resurrection, the original apostles wrote most of the books of the New Testament. Both their experience and mission were unique and unrepeatable.

In a more general sense, however, an apostle is simply a representative or mes-senger. In addition to the special group just noted, the New Testament calls others "apostles of the churches" (2 Cor 8:23), two of whom Paul greets at the end of his letter to the church in Rome (Rom 16:7). The term can also be used for any special messenger or missionary (Phil 2:25).

Prophecy also serves a broader function than revelation of new truth to become inspired Scripture. Joel predicted that in the messianic age the Spirit would be poured out on all people for them to prophesy (Joel 2:28). Peter explained the events of Pentecost as a fulfillment of that prophecy (Acts 2:14-21). Paul taught the church at Corinth, "You can all prophesy in turn so that everyone may be instructed and encour-aged" (1 Cor 14:31). Prophetic messages are given by the Spirit for the "strengthening, encouragement and comfort" (1 Cor 14:3) of a local church in a specific situation.

So in this more general sense the church in every age needs the ministry of apostles and prophets, along with that of evangelists, pastors and teachers who bring people into the church and build them up in the faith.

Study 4. Power for Mission. Acts 1:1-11; 2:1-13.

Purpose: To discover how Jesus kept his promise to empower the disciples and to help us participate in the mission begun at Pentecost.

Question 2. You may wish to ask the group to read through Acts 1:1-11 silently.

Question 4. The Jews of that day expected a Messiah who would re-establish King David's throne by overthrowing their enemies. Although Jesus had not taught his disciples that concept of his mission, they still clung to the age-old Jewish hope of a restored political kingdom.

Questions 9-10. Pentecost was celebrated fifty days after Passover. Marking the end of the spring harvest, the ceremony on Pentecost offered the first two loaves of new grain. It was one of the three great pilgrimage festivals which required Israel's attendance at the temple (Deut 16:16). So Jerusalem was thronged with pilgrims from other parts of the Roman Empire.

The phrase *filled with the Spirit* belongs especially to Luke, who uses it in his Gospel and Acts seven of the eight times it occurs in the New Testament. (It is used once by Paul in Ephesians 5:18.) *Filled with the Spirit* consistently connotes an immediate action of the Holy Spirit to produce results that can be witnessed—seen or heard, for which Paul generally uses the term *spiritual gift* (see 1 Cor 14:26; Eph 5:18-24; Col 3:16). Here in Acts 2:4 *filled with the Spirit* is a synonym for Jesus' phrase *clothed with power from on high* (Lk 24:49), his promise to the disciples before he left them, which he equates with *baptize with the Spirit* (Acts 1:4-5).

Question 11. The pilgrims did not require this miraculous phenomenon in order to understand the disciples' message, since they all spoke Aramaic or Greek. But for this occasion speaking "in other tongues" served both a practical and a symbolic purpose. Practically it brought together a crowd perplexed and curious to learn more about what was happening. This speaking in foreign languages was also a sign of God's purpose to proclaim the good news of Christ not only in Jerusalem but also "to the ends of the earth" (Acts 1:8). In the providence of God the nations of the world were represented by those God-fearing Jews gathered in Jerusalem. That event was a preview of the church's mission over the miles and throughout the years. For some this phenomenon also served to authenticate the apostles' message.

Study 5. Evangelism. Acts 2:14-41.

Purpose: To understand the significance of Pentecost, the essentials of the gospel and how we can effectively communicate the message of Christ.

Question 2. For dramatic effect you may want to have one member volunteer to give Peter's sermon and another take the role of David for the quotations from his psalms (vv. 14-36).

Question 7. Peter's audience of devout Jews had a high regard for their Old Testament Scriptures, whose prophets looked forward to a new messianic age. Joel had predicted such an outpouring of God's Spirit. King David's psalm spoke of the resurrection of the Messiah, God's anointed (the "Christ"). Peter used those scriptures to gain a hearing for his message.

Question 10. Luke records three central and related elements involved in becoming a Christian: repentance, water-baptism and the reception of the Holy Spirit. Peter's three verbs are *repent, baptize* and *receive*. Two of these verbs are commands and one is a promise. Repentance is the sinner's active response to the gospel; water-baptism is performed by the Christian community; the gift of the Holy Spirit is received from God.

It is important to note that Luke presents no standard formula for conversion. In the following chapters he varies the sequence and sometimes omits one of these elements in his narrative. This practice is understandable in light of the author's purpose: to record the growth and expansion of the church, not steps in the personal spiritual life of the disciples.

Note on the Significance of Pentecost. Differing interpretations of the meaning of Pentecost for the disciples and the church have made this passage one of the most controversial in the New Testament. Much of the debate centers on the phrase *baptize in [with, by] the Spirit*. An understanding of this chapter must be based on several basic principles.

1. Luke is a theologian as well as a historian. In other words, his historical narrative presents a specific teaching about the role of the Holy Spirit in the growth of the church.

2. A given word or phrase can have more than one meaning. In each case the meaning is found in the context and way the word or phrase is used. Most discussions of *baptize in the Spirit* fail to recognize the possibility that it can have more than one meaning.

This phrase was originally used by two different men: John the Baptist and the apostle Paul. John told the crowds that Jesus would "baptize with the Holy Spirit." That statement is reported in all four Gospels: Mt 3:11; Mk 1:8; Lk 3:16; Jn 1:33. Shortly before Pentecost, Jesus quoted that phrase and equated it with his promise that the disciples would be "clothed with power from on high" for their mission (Lk 24:49; Acts 1:4-5). That experience was defined and applied by Jesus as an action of the Holy Spirit that empowered his disciples for mission or service. Peter also quoted his Lord's use of this phrase in connection with the Holy Spirit's being poured out on the household of Cornelius (Acts 10:44-46; 11:15-17). In Luke's Pentecost narrative, *baptize with the Spirit* meant *filled with the Spirit* to powerfully proclaim the good news of Christ.

Paul used the phrase *baptized by one Spirit* with an entirely different meaning, to describe the individual's incorporation into the body of Christ at the beginning of the Christian life (1 Cor 12:13). The context is the salvation of the Corinthians at the beginning of their Christian life. That meaning should not be imported into Acts 2 and imposed on Luke's report of the disciples' first public service.

3. Finally, Pentecost had different meanings for those involved. For Jesus, in addition to his resurrection, it marked the vindication of his rejected claims and ministry. For the disciples, Pentecost provided the promised power for their mission and the establishment of a strong, effective Christian community. (The disciples had already received the Holy Spirit in the upper room—see John 20:22.) For the three thousand, this day marked their initial reception of the Holy Spirit and their membership into this community.

Study 6. Teaching & Preaching. Acts 18:1-28.

Purpose: To learn how Paul manifested the gift of teaching to multiply his influence through those he discipled.

Question 2. Have individuals take turns reading the passage aloud, one paragraph at a time.

Question 4. Unlike the Greek philosophers and rulers, the Jews did not despise manual labor. Every rabbi had a trade with which he could support himself.

Question 10. Apollos came from Egypt, where Alexandria was the second most important city in the Roman Empire and had a large Jewish population.

Question 11. As a follow-up question, you might ask the group what they think it meant for Priscilla and Aquila to teach Apollos "the way of God more adequately" (v. 26).

Study 7. Healing (Part 1). Mark 1:21-45; James 5:13-20.

Purpose: To understand the importance of healing in Jesus' ministry and its practice in the church. (In the first eight chapters Mark devotes about equal space to teaching and healing.)

Question 4. Since the Jewish Sabbath extended from sunset to sunset, this gathering of people at the home of Peter and Andrew took place after it had officially ended. Many Jewish leaders regarded healing activitiy on the Sabbath as a violation of God's law (see Mk 3:1-6).

Question 5. Jesus was not given an advance schedule for his ministry. Each day, led by the Spirit (Lk 4:1), he had to decide whether to remain where he was or go to another place. Note the difficult decision he had to make one day when he heard that his friend Lazarus was very ill (Jn 11:1-6).

Question 6. According to the law of Moses, anyone with leprosy could not touch or be touched by another person and was ostracized from normal human contacts (Lev 13:9-11).

Question 8. Have volunteers read the three paragraphs.

Question 9. In 1 Corinthians 12:9 we noted that Paul uses the phrase *gifts of healings,* a double plural that indicates a variety of illness and different means of healing. James expects in this case that the needed healing will come through the prayer and anointing by the church elders. Today a physical, emotional or spiritual illness can be healed by a variety of gifts; for example, prayer, anointing, counseling, medicine, surgery— singly or in combination, as the Spirit determines.

Study 8. Healing (Part 2). John 21:1-19.

Purpose: To realize the Lord's power and desire to heal all memories of past hurts and emotional wounds.

Question 2. Ask for volunteers to take the parts of the narrator, Jesus, Peter and (one person) the rest of the disciples.

Question 6. For the background of this story, have a member read aloud the passages mentioned in the question, with the group listening (not reading the passage in their own Bibles).

The word for *fire*, which refers to a charcoal fire, appears only one other place in the New Testament—at the trial of Jesus in John 18:18, where Peter denied his Lord. Note also the present setting of beach and fishing similar to that of Peter's first call to be a disciple in Mark 1:14-20.

Study 9. Prophecy & Tongues. 1 Corinthians 14.

Purpose: To understand the purpose and proper use of the gifts of prophecy and speaking in tongues, so that corporate worship may be conducted in a fitting and orderly way.

Question 2. This question is designed to give an overview of the chapter before encountering the detailed arguments. The group may either read it silently or aloud by paragraphs, depending on which seems to be more suitable at this point. Paul sums up the preceding two chapters in verse 1: "Follow the way of love and eagerly desire spiritual gifts." It is important to recognize that the command *eagerly desire* is in the plural form, addressed to the entire church and not to the individual who might be overeager to have certain gifts manifested through him or her.

Questions 3-4. Much of the difficulty in understanding Paul's teaching in this chapter lies in the style of argument. It is a letter sharing elements of his own experience as well as illustrations from life. Keep in mind that the key to understanding this teaching is given in verse 14: "Unless you speak *intelligible words* with your tongue, how will anyone know what you are saying?" Gifts of inspired speech must be understood if they are to build up the body of Christ. For this reason, a message in tongues in a public meeting must also have the companion gift of interpretation.

Prophecy in the Bible is essentially a direct message from God evaluating a specific situation and calling for a response. Often prophecy also foretells future events, but this element is usually not its main purpose.

Paul criticizes speaking in tongues in groups only when it goes uninterpreted. The central issue of this discussion is *intelligibility* (14:19). If we understand a message we can profit from it; without this understanding we are not edified. When interpreted, this gift has the same value as prophecy since the message can be understood (14:5b). Thus it has a place with prophecy in the model of public worship (14:26-35). Speaking in tongues with interpretation, like prophecy, is also valuable for the "strengthening, encouragement and comfort" of the church (14:3, 26, 31).

Question 7. The statement in verses 21-22 is difficult to understand and has given rise to several different interpretations. When Israel was disobedient, God sent them prophets speaking in their own language. When they refused to listen to God, he sent foreigners, in that case the invading Assyrians, whose language they could not understand (see Mt 13:10-15). The lesson is that unbelievers will be sent unintelligible teachers, while believers will be sent those who can be understood. The main point to keep in mind, however, is Paul's concern that a public message in tongues should be interpreted so that the church can profit from its message.

Question 8. Paul's teaching about the manifestation of spiritual gifts does not focus primarily on the experience of the individual but the need of the church (v. 26). All of these must be done for the "strengthening of the church."

Notice also that the gifts are not for a select few individuals or church offices. Paul says, "I would like everyone of you to speak in tongues, but would rather you prophesy" (v. 4). "For you can all prophesy in turn so that everyone may be instructed and encouraged" (v. 31). In verse 26 he recognizes a diversity of gifts coming through different people in the worship service as the Spirit enables.

Question 10. Paul's instructions in verses 27-35 insure that those who wish to speak in church will be monitored so that the church may profit and order may be kept.

In this long chapter, there isn't time to discuss verses 34-36 in detail. Although the subject of women in the church is important, the issue cannot be settled from this passage alone. It should be noted, however, that Paul expected women as well as men to pray and prophesy in public worship (11:5).

Study 10. Various Spiritual Gifts. Romans 12:1-16.
Purpose: To understand how commitment to God and an accurate appraisal of ourselves can help us to function well as members of the body of Christ.

Question 5. Like the list in our first study (1 Cor 12:8-10), this one appears to be a random sample. While in Paul's lists the first item sometimes has special importance for the immediate context, the sequence itself cannot be taken as an order of rank. Last place can be a position of prominence (for example, showing mercy, one of the great attributes of God. See Ex 23:6-7). Paul makes no distinction between what we consider "natural" (serving, encouraging) and "supernatural" (prophesying), as if only the latter were a special activity of the Spirit (see Appendix A).

The Greek word for *service* (v. 7) means any kind of service. For example, kitchen duty after a church supper, if it is motivated by a desire to serve the fellowship, is just as much a spiritual gift as giving a prophecy.

Question 6. The difference between natural abilities and spiritual gifts is often overlooked. A natural ability or aptitude, like music or physical coordination, is an inherent personal characteristic often evident from childhood. It can be developed and used as the individual decides, selfishly or for the glory of God. A charism or spiritual gift, however, is a manifestation of the Holy Spirit to meet a specific need for the common good (1 Cor 12:7); for example, a word of encouragement or healing or financial contribution.

A spiritual gift received by the body of Christ may involve the use of a natural ability. A teaching may be given by a scholar with special aptitude for study and communication. A song of encouragement may come from a member with musical talent. On the other hand, many spiritual gifts do not require innate abilities (1 Cor 12:8-10). For example, a word of wisdom doesn't depend on a high IQ, nor a message in tongues on linguistic ability, nor an act of mercy on a compassionate disposition.

But whether or not a member's special ability is involved, a spiritual gift (like a birthday present) is essentially evident in the giving and receiving of the body of Christ to empower its worship, service or witness. It is an event that can be seen or heard and appreciated, an evidence of the presence and power of the Holy Spirit.

The New Testament does not distinguish between what we call "natural" and "supernatural" gifts. An act of mercy or service in repairing the church can be just as much a manifestation of the Spirit as a word of knowledge or healing we cannot explain. If one of the members is out of work, generously give money and not a prophecy!

Traditional theology and American individualism have fostered a self-centered approach to spiritual gifts. We are frequently urged to enquire, "What is my gift? How can I discover and use it?" This introspective approach often leads to preoccupation with when and how "my gift" will be used. As a corrective we should rather focus on the needs of the Christian community and be ready to respond as the Spirit leads. Over a period of time you may discover that you are being "gifted" in a certain way. Recognition and encouragement comes from the body which as a result is being built up.

Study 11. The Fruit of the Spirit. Galatians 5:13-26.

Purpose: To understand the importance of the fruit of the Spirit in our character, along with the gifts of the Spirit in our worship and service. (See Appendix B, pp. 63-64.)

Question 2. Have people take turns reading the passage aloud, one paragraph at a time.

Question 3. Paul uses the word *law* in several ways. In verse 13 the "entire law" is all of the Ten Commandments and other requirements for righteous living given in the Old Testament. In verse 18 the expression *not under law* does not mean freedom from keeping God's commands; rather it is freedom from the impossible burden of keeping all these laws in order to earn our salvation. In verse 23 *law* is used simply as a prohibition, whether religious or civil.

Question 10. This does not mean that we become completely free from all sin, but rather that it no longer has its old power over us. Paul's wording indicates that this "crucifixion" occurred at our conversion to Christ.

Study 12. The Excellent Way of Love. 1 Corinthians 13.

Purpose: To understand the meaning and importance of love in the manifestation of spiritual gifts and in our relationships with others.

Question 2. Get several volunteers to read through the passage in turn, one paragraph at a time.

The last half of 1 Corinthians 12:31 can be translated "the way of excellence" or "the excellent way." Paul does not teach that love is a *better way* than spiritual gifts; it is the *only way* these gifts are manifested with any value at all.

Furthermore, love is not a gift, not even the greatest of gifts. In the New Testament love is listed as a fruit of the Spirit. (See Galatians 5:22-23, where it comes first.) Love is the underlying motive and method for manifesting all spiritual gifts since it is not self-centered but rather focuses on others and the needs of the body.

Question 6. In these verses Paul teaches that a time will come when the gifts of prophecy, tongues and knowledge will no longer be needed. He calls it the "perfection," which is sometimes interpreted to mean the completion of the New Testament at the end of the first century, after which revelational gifts are no longer needed. That view has three major difficulties.

First, Paul describes the perfection as the time when "we shall see face to face" and "know fully, even as I am fully known"; that is, perfectly (13:12). But that condition did not exist at the end of the apostolic age. Second, this view narrows the function of these gifts to the few apostles and prophets through whom inspired Scripture was written. Paul teaches, however, a wider continuing purpose for these gifts, potentially manifested by all in the church for its "strengthening, comfort and encouragement" (1 Cor 14:3-5, 26, 31). Third, these three gifts, along with others, including healing and miracles, actually continued for several centuries. But they gradually waned as the church became worldly, especially after Constantine's recognition of Christianity gave it political status. Therefore, the perfection must refer to a future time, whether the death of the Christian or the return of Christ, when the gifts will no longer be needed since all imperfection will have disappeared.

Charles Hummel is the faculty specialist for InterVarsity Christian Fellowship and the author of several books, including Fire in the Fireplace *and* The Galileo Connection *(both from IVP). He and his wife, Anne, have extensive experience in Bible study groups and are the authors of the* LifeGuide Genesis: God's Creative Call.

Appendix A: New Testament Gift Lists

The New Testament has nine lists of gifts, eight of which appear in the writings of Paul. Of the latter, six consist of spiritual gifts (Rom 12:6-8; 1 Cor 12:8-10; 13:1-3; 13:8; 14:6; 14:26); one comprises gifted individuals (Eph 4:11); and one has both categories (1 Cor 12:28). Peter's list consists of spiritual gifts (1 Pet 4:9-11).

It is commonly assumed that the biblical writers provide an order of rank, so that the relative value of a gift can be determined by its place on a list. Thus, prophecy and wisdom are to be considered most important because they often appear first, while speaking in tongues is the least of the spiritual gifts because it comes last (Rom 12:6-8; 1 Cor 12:8-10). But this assumption is valid only if the context and usage show that the author intends to list the gifts in order of rank. Otherwise such an evaluation by commentators reflects their own view more than that of the biblical writer. (For example, biblical scholars who consider tongues to be least because listed last in 1 Corinthians 12:8-10, 29-30 do not conclude that their own gift of teaching is of least importance because it appears last in Ephesians 4:11.)

The following brief analysis examines the way spiritual gifts are listed and how their order may be properly understood.

Ephesians 4:11 Apostles, prophets, evangelists, pastors, teachers.

In Ephesians Paul stresses the importance of the founding role played by the first apostles and prophets in the church (Eph 2:20; 3:5). Evangelists then preach the gospel and bring others into the Christian community. Pastors and teachers provide the ongoing nurture and guidance needed by the new converts as well as the older believers. The list of gifted individuals in Ephesians 4:11 seems to indicate something of a chronological order in the initial establishment of the church and subsequent Christian communities. There is no evidence, however, that Paul considers evangelists more important than pastors in any absolute sense or that teachers are of least importance because they are listed last.

Romans 12:6-8 Prophesying, serving, teaching, encouraging, contributing, leading, showing mercy.

Prophecy is prominent in Paul's teaching and appears early on most of his lists. The other gifts show no order of rank.

Mercy, for example, can hardly be considered least important just because it comes last. It appears that this list is a random selection of spiritual gifts of speech and action illustrating the diverse functions of members in the same body.

1 Corinthians 12:8-10 Wisdom, knowledge, faith, healings, miracles, prophecy, discerning of spirits, speaking in tongues, interpretation of tongues.

Wisdom and knowledge are involved in the most serious problem at Corinth, to which Paul devotes most of the first four chapters. The next three are spiritual gifts of action which are not prominent in this letter. The last two pairs involve inspired speech and figure prominently in Paul's instruction in 1 Corinthians 14.

The three groups do not evidence an absolute order of rank. Within each group the first word appears to be key: *wisdom* involves knowledge; *faith* is basic to healings and miracles; speaking in tongues with interpretation is a form of *prophecy*. If there is an order, it seems to be one of degree of misuse, since this is a problem-oriented letter. First and last place on a list or in a sentence can be positions of emphasis. Both wisdom (first) and tongues (last) were being misused at Corinth.

1 Corinthians 12:28 First apostles, second prophets, third teachers, then miracles, then gifts of healings, helpful deeds, administrations, different kinds of tongues.

The ranking of gifted individuals is obvious; this is the only list in which Paul assigns an explicit order of importance. The following five spiritual gifts appear to be a random sample of action and speech, three appearing in 1 Corinthians 12:8-10 and two similar to the gifts in Romans 12.

Notice that only the *gifted individuals* are explicitly ranked. It is not clear why, among the spiritual gifts, miracles and healings come first. As valuable as they are, these two are not necessarily the most important for every occasion. Here also the pattern is a random illustration of diversity, rather than an order of rank.

This same illustration of diversity is evident in the four brief lists of 1 Corinthians 13 and 14.

13:1-3	13:8	14:6	14:26
tongues	prophecies	revelation	instruction
prophecy	tongues	knowledge	revelation
knowledge	knowledge	prophecy	tongues
faith		teaching	interpretation

Most of these spiritual gifts involve speech and knowledge, which are important in building up the body. Since the context in chapter 14 is public worship, this focus on gifts of speech is understandable. In these four brief lists, the same gifts do not appear in any consistent order. Sometimes, for example, tongues is first, sometimes it appears second or third. It is evident that Paul does not intend to teach the relative value of spiritual gifts by the place they occupy on a list.

1 Peter 4:9-11 Hospitality, prophecy, service.

Hospitality without grumbling, speaking the very words of God and serving with the strength God provides are all spiritual gifts. The context of this list and the order of the gifts show no intent to assign value according to place. Like Paul, Peter uses a random sample to illustrate his teaching that the gifts should be used in love "to serve others, faithfully administering God's grace in its various forms" (4:10).

Conclusion Our study of these lists of spiritual gifts shows that Paul consistently selects and orders gifts randomly in order to illustrate diversity, rather than to indicate rank. Where there appears to be a logical order, it must be understood in the context of the passage and not made an absolute for all occasions. This pattern is consistent with Paul's doctrine of the body, wherein each member serves a meaningful function according to the needs of the community, not according to a hierarchical ladder of status. Every charism, as a manifestation of the Spirit for the common good, is valuable as it strengthens the body in its own way at the right time. No one member or gift is most important at all times; this prominence belongs only to the Head. It is not surprising, therefore, that attempts to rank a gift according to its place on the list are subjective at best. For example, scholars who give the lowest value to speaking in tongues because it appears last in 1 Corinthians 12, fail to draw the same conclusion about their own gift of teaching in Ephesians 4:11. Furthermore, these lists provide no basis for the frequently used categories of *natural* and *supernatural, permanent* and *temporary, ordinary* and *spectacular, normal* and *abnormal, usual* and *unusual.* We should not impose on the text these unbiblical categories derived from our experience. The last two distinctions are statistical terms based on the status quo. They reflect the current experience of the church more than the standard of biblical teaching on which our doctrine and practice of spiritual gifts should be based.The charismatic renewal calls for a return to the New Testament model of the church in which members of the body exercise the full range of spiritual gifts for worship, witness and service.

Charles E. Hummel, "Appendix B: Notes on New Testament Gift Lists," *Fire in the Fireplace* (InterVarsity Press, 1978), pp. 243-46.

Appendix B: The Charismatic Dimension

Two dimensions of the Spirit's activity in the Christian's life have long been recognized. At the beginning, according to Jesus, we are *born again* by the Spirit (Jn 3:5). Or as Paul puts it, God "saved us . . . by the washing of *regeneration* and *renewal* in the Holy Spirit" (Tit 3:5 RSV). As a result, the believer is "in Christ, he is a *new creation"* (2 Cor 5:17). This is not simply an individual experience: "We were all *baptized by one Spirit* into one body" (1 Cor 12:13). As members of this body we are united with each other in Christ who is the Head.

The second dimension of the Holy Spirit's activity involves the development of this new life. Christians are called to *sanctification,* that is, growth in holiness. "It is God's will that you should be *holy.* . . . May God himself, the God of peace, *sanctify* you through and through" (1 Thess 4:3; 5:23). Paul urges Christians to turn from evil so that they will be instruments "for noble purposes, *made holy,* useful to the Master and prepared to do any good work" (2 Tim 2:21). The Spirit empowers us to make ethical and moral decisions, sometimes costly, in a life of maturing love for God and our neighbors. He also develops in us the *fruit* of the Spirit, which is Christlike character.

Traditionally, spiritual gifts have been considered an aspect of sanctification—individual abilities or talents to be discovered and developed to serve the Lord. But our study shows that the manifestation of spiritual gifts involves something quite different. It is a third dimension of the Holy Spirit's activity, through members with varying degrees of maturity, to meet specific needs of the body. While this charismatic action may utilize an individual's ability, often it does not.

Luke gives primary emphasis to the Holy Spirit's role in bringing the messianic age and expanding the church. Filling with the Spirit empowers Christians to carry out their Lord's commission to preach the gospel to all nations. Paul, on the other hand, emphasizes the role of the Spirit in building the body of Christ. Therefore he gives special attention to the place of spiritual gifts in inspiring worship and strengthening the Christian community.

Yet both writers stress the charismatic dimension of the Holy Spirit's activity as an immediate action to produce specific results. Something happens that can be heard or seen, whether a prophecy or word of wisdom, a healing or act of mercy. There is an event which manifests or gives evidence of the Spirit's power.

Neither Luke nor Paul considers this experience as *another stage* of spiritual maturity. In Acts mature Christians were repeatedly filled to empower their witness and service. As Joel foretold, the Spirit was poured out on young and old, men and women. In 1 Corinthians 12 Paul emphasizes that each member of the body manifests some gift for the *common good.* The focus is on activity which benefits the church. This charismatic dimension of the Spirit's activity repeatedly empowers the Christian at *every stage* of spiritual growth to be effective for the Lord in the church and the world.

Fruit of the Spirit

The distinctions between the fruit and gifts of the Spirit are sometimes blurred. Often one is elevated at the expense of the other. So we need to be clear about their differences and the way they relate to each other.

Paul writes: "But the fruit of the Spirit is love, joy, peace, patience, kindness, goodness, faithfulness, gentleness and self-control" (Gal 5:22-23). These words describe a quality of life. In the last analysis, the value of all we *do* depends on the kind of people we *are.*

The first distinction is between being and doing, character and action. The fruit of the Spirit describes the kind of people Christians should *be:* loving, joyful, patient, self-controlled. On the other hand, the gifts of the Spirit describe what believers *do* as members of the body of Christ: teaching, serving, speaking a word of wisdom or healing.

Second, the fruit is Christlike character which the Spirit desires to produce in all Christians. No one may say, "Don't expect me to love; that isn't my fruit." Everyone is to bear all the fruit. But spiritual gifts are just the opposite. Members of the body exercise different gifts as the Spirit distributes them.

Third, while the fruit of the Spirit is meant for all times and places, spiritual gifts are given for specific needs. We should expect spiritual fruit from Christians on all occasions. But we cannot predict or program the gifts of the Spirit.

Paul neither blurs these distinctions nor severs the connection between fruit and gifts. The fruit of the Spirit does not appear in his lists of spiritual gifts, although he does expect these gifts to be exercised in love and with self-control. Some Christians emphasize spiritual gifts with insufficient concern for spiritual fruit. Others claim that the real evidence of the Spirit's filling is Christian character. But Paul does not offer us a choice. Both the fruit and the gifts of the Spirit are necessary for the church's health and effectiveness.

Christ and the Spirit

The manifestation of spiritual gifts is not an experience "beyond Christ" either. Throughout the New Testament the actions of the Spirit and the work of Christ are intertwined. If justification is Christ's righteousness provided *for* us, regeneration his life given *to* us, and sanctification his character formed *in* us, then, filling with the Spirit or manifestation of spiritual gifts is Christ's activity *through* us to strengthen the body and fulfill its mission in the world.

Above all we must focus on Jesus Christ. When we have trouble thinking about the Spirit, or get bogged down with introspection about what we call *our* gifts, let us look to our Lord, who is always related to the Spirit's activity. The following questions may help.

1. *Is my life increasingly under the lordship of Christ in terms of goals and daily decisions?* Through the Spirit we confess "Jesus is Lord" not only at conversion but also as a way of living.

2. *Am I becoming more like Jesus in my attitudes and reactions to others?* The fruit of the Spirit is Christlike character being formed in us.

3. *Are my moral and ethical decisions those which Jesus Christ our Lord would make?* The Spirit desires to make us holy and useful in the service of our Lord.

4. *Am I participating in a Christian fellowship, concerned for others and open to the Spirit's work through me to meet their needs?* The gifts of the Spirit are manifestations of his power through members of the body of Christ to empower the church's worship, witness and service.

As we live under the lordship of Christ individually and corporately, we can look for the Spirit's filling, anointing, empowering as the occasion requires and he determines. While we may disagree about which spiritual gifts to expect, let us serve our Lord Jesus Christ together with this resolve: "In essentials, unity; in nonessentials, diversity; and in all things, charity (love)."

Excerpts from Charles E. Hummel, *Filled with the Spirit* (InterVarsity Press, 1981), pp. 20-25, 30-32.